Try Not To Laugh Challenge
BONUS PLAY

Join our Joke Club and get the Bonus Play PDF!

Simply send us an email to:

TNTLPublishing@gmail.com

and you will get the following:

- 10 Hilarious Would You Rather Questions
- An entry in our Monthly Giveaway of a $50 Amazon Gift card!

We draw a new winner each month and will contact you via email!

Good luck!

Welcome to the Try Not to Laugh Challenge "Would You Rather?" Book!

◆

Read a Would You Rather Question to yourself or aloud to a friend, then pick between the two options! Sometimes it's easy, but sometimes it's not... Explanations of answers are always encouraged! If playing with a friend, pass it back and forth to keep the game going! Enjoy!

REMEMBER, these scenarios listed in the book are solely for fun and games! Please do <u>NOT</u> attempt any of the crazy scenarios in this book.

Would You Rather?

Would you rather hang on the monkey bars for 20 minutes OR climb a 500-foot tree?

Would you rather take a mud bath OR an icicle shower?

Would you rather be able to speak and understand 3 languages OR have the ability to understand all languages, but not speak it?

Would you rather have ALL your food taste really sweet OR have it taste really salty?

Would you rather have a can of live worms poured on you OR have multiple pieces of gum stuck in your hair, at once?

Would you rather have to fight 50 ant-sized alligators OR 1 alligator-sized ant?

Would you rather wear 40 shirts at once, on the hottest day of summer OR wear one incredibly itchy sweater for an hour?

Would you rather have three noses and be able to sing beautifully OR have a giant mouth, but only talk in whispers?

Would you rather wear a beard of crawling ants for a full day OR speak backwards for a week?

Would you rather be able to play any instrument perfectly, but have five arms OR wear a bicycle helmet that makes your head look 5x smaller?

Would you rather have a cactus as a tongue OR turn into a giant lizard every year, on your birthday?

Would you rather have bubbles come out of your mouth every time you speak OR live in a whale's stomach for a year?

Would you rather have the ability to fly, but only 2 feet off the ground OR be a genius, but only for 30 minutes a day?

Would you rather sneeze every time someone says the word "the", OR fart every time someone says the word "and"?

Would you rather shoot lasers out of your eyes OR have the ability to transform into any animal?

Would you rather eat cake-flavored toothpaste OR toothpaste-flavored cake?

Would you rather go sky-diving OR zip-lining, through a jungle?

Would you rather eat a burger with a side of dog treats OR dog food with a side of fries?

Would you rather own a dog that could talk like a human OR a plant that made infinite ice cream?

Would you rather grow a second set of arms, so you could hold twice as many things, OR grow a second set of legs, so you could run twice as fast?

Would you rather have a tongue like a lizard OR eyes like a cat?

Would you rather be able to eat anything and not gain excess weight OR play sports and never need to shower?

Would you rather walk a mile in a blizzard OR spend a day in the world's hottest desert?

Would you rather have a smartphone implanted in your arm OR only be able to use an old-fashion corded phone?

Would you rather have to talk using a puppet OR speak in a squeaky voice all the time?

———————◆———————

Would you rather be able to jump as high as a building OR swim as deep as a blue whale?

Would you rather have
X-ray vision OR the ability
to hypnotize people?

Would you rather have
your bottom where your
nose is OR your nose
where your bottom is?

Would you rather dress as a duster and clean a tomato juice covered bathroom floor, OR clean a dumpster filled with marshmallows, using only a toothbrush?

Would you rather see ghosts all the time OR live in a haunted house and only see ghosts sometimes?

Would you rather meet an alien from Mars, OR meet someone famous from Earth?

Would you rather be lost inside a zoo where all the wild animals roam free OR accidentally go swimming in the shark tank of an aquarium?

Would you rather only be able to wash your face and body with a tortilla shell OR only be able to brush your hair with two lobster claws?

Would you rather only eat salty food for the rest of your life OR only eat sour food?

Would you rather always have an annoying song stuck in your head OR always think you hear someone calling your name?

Would you rather be able to stop time OR be able to speed it up?

Would you rather speak only in rhymes OR talk only in riddles?

Would you rather spend 3 hours jumping on a trampoline non-stop OR run 3 miles through the woods?

Would you rather have a tiny pet dinosaur OR a giant pet squirrel?

Would you rather be chained to a rhino in a stampede OR be tied to a shark swimming at TOP speed?

Would you rather live in a shell like a turtle OR live in a nest like a bird?

Would you rather walk barefoot across a floor covered in LEGO's or walk barefoot across hot coals?

Would you rather live in a fictional world, OR bring a fictional character into our world?

Would you rather live in the same place forever, OR move somewhere different every year?

Would you rather be as big as a skyscraper OR as small as a flea?

Would you rather turn into a werewolf one week/per month OR walk around with a wolf tail forever?

Would you rather have teeth like a rabbit OR no teeth at all?

Would you rather hang upside down by your toes, OR hang right side up by your ears?

Would you rather have hair that can change colors OR skin that can change colors?

Would you rather have all your choices be made by other people OR by flipping a coin?

Would you rather bark like a dog OR caw like a bird, at the end of every sentence you say?

Would you rather take a bath in barbecue sauce OR a shower in ketchup?

Would you rather have a car that could fly OR a bicycle car that turned into a submarine?

Would you rather the sky always be black and white, OR your dreams were all black and white?

Would you rather always run out of toilet paper OR live in a house made out of toilet paper?

———————◆———————

Would you rather walk through a field of snakes OR have a backpack full of slugs?

Would you rather be able to explore the inside of an active volcano OR the sun?

———◆———

Would you rather have to eat an extremely sour lemon OR an extremely hot jalapeño pepper?

Would you rather have glittery black blood OR neon glowing tears?

Would you rather be 2 feet tall and super strong OR 8 feet tall and really fast?

Would you rather have to sing everything you say, OR not be able to speak at all?

Would you rather sleep on a bed of broccoli for a month, OR on a bed of dirty diapers for a day?

Would you rather be able to breathe underwater, but have fish fins for arms OR have the power of invisibility, but every time you turn invisible you fart loudly?

Would you rather have buttons for eyes OR ride on a slimy slug to school every day?

Would you rather only be able to tell lies for the rest of your life, OR only be able to speak the truth?

Would you rather have a cheese block-shaped head OR skin like a cheetah?

Would you rather fly on a Pterodactyl, OR ride on a Tyrannosaurus Rex?

Would you rather go backward in time when you sneeze OR advance to the future when you cough?

Would you rather eat as many candy bars as you want, but have to read a book every week, OR watch as many movies as you want, but only eat steamed broccoli?

Would you rather hug a hungry alligator OR wash your clothes in a tub full of angry crabs?

Would you rather squeeze lemon juice into a paper cut OR use toilet paper made from tree bark?

Would you rather eat a vegetable you hate, every day OR eat a potato bug once?

Would you rather go on a merry-go-round for 6 hours straight OR be chased by evil robots?

Would you rather have the speed of a turtle, but super strength OR be the smartest person alive, but talk like a duck?

Would you rather live in the time of dinosaurs OR have the dinosaurs live in our time?

Would you rather get around by only doing cartwheels, OR by having to crawl on your hands and knees?

Would you rather have an elephant's trunk OR a pig's nose?

———————◆———————

Would you rather run through a field of scorpions OR run through a house full of hornets?

Would you rather fall into a muddy puddle face first OR slip on a banana peel in front of everyone?

Would you rather be really hairy like Big Foot OR bald like a naked mole rat?

Would you rather eat a lollipop covered in dog fur OR a chocolate covered worm?

Would you rather never taste sugar again OR never eat your favorite food again?

Would you rather sleep with a 2-foot snake in your bed OR 2,000 fire ants?

Would you rather have a twin you can switch places with OR a robot that does all your work?

Would you rather talk in an opera singing voice OR only be able to rap when you talk?

Would you rather be able to live on the moon OR be able to live on Mars?

Would you rather have an extra-large head and normal sized body OR a normal sized head and a giant-sized body?

Would you rather have teeth made from corn OR have a nose made from a slice of cake?

Would you rather eat a donut filled with mayo OR a cupcake filled with relish?

———————◆———————

Would you rather climb Mount Everest in a swimsuit, OR walk through the Sahara Desert in full winter clothes?

Would you rather have cooked noodles for fingers OR raw chicken nuggets for toes?

Would you rather control your dreams OR control your friend's dreams?

Would you rather have to eat broccoli with every meal OR not be able to eat french fries ever again?

Would you rather attend school all year and never have homework OR go to school for 2 months and have homework, all year?

Would you rather sneeze brussel sprouts OR cry hot sauce?

Would you rather plant a garden of Venus flytraps OR take care of an active beehive?

Would you rather do the chicken dance OR sing a lullaby at your school's talent show?

———————◆———————

Would you rather be able to see through walls OR walk through them?

Would you rather have hands that could stick to anything OR feet that had wheels on them?

Would you rather be a caterpillar that turned into a butterfly OR a snail that turned into a cobra?

Would you rather laugh every time you heard something sad OR cry every time you heard good news?

Would you rather live in a mansion alone OR in a tent with your favorite celebrities?

Would you rather always
be hungry, but can only
eat dirt OR always
be thirsty, but can only
drink soapy water?

Would you rather
communicate telepathically
OR secretly read minds?

Would you rather have a tiny dinosaur for a pet OR a giant house-sized dog?

Would you rather have to wear underwear on your head for a month, OR wear underwear over your pants for a year?

Would you rather shrink to be a foot tall, but become the smartest person ever, OR be so strong you can lift a house, but are only able to talk by burping?

Would rather have to hug a smelly monkey OR kiss a muddy pig?

Would you rather bathe in a bathtub full of broccoli and cheese soup OR tan yourself with barbecue sauce?

Would you rather ride a rollercoaster with no seatbelt and/or brakes, OR hang from a chairlift with no net, as it moves up a mountain?

Would you rather have a genie OR be a genie?

Would you rather eat bacon-flavored ice cream OR hot sauce-flavored ice cream?

Would you rather shower for three hours every day for the rest of your life, OR never shower again?

Would you rather have an infinite supply of cookies, but they're all oatmeal raisin OR an infinite supply of cakes, but they're all carrot cake?

Would you rather always look like you have lettuce in your teeth, OR always smell like peanut butter?

Would you rather own a cat that acts like a dog OR a dog that acts like a cat?

Would you rather walk on your hands to get to places, OR crabwalk everywhere?

Would you rather hiccup every 2 minutes for the rest of your life, OR have to give a speech to a full room with very loud gas?

Would you rather have everything with a screen break when you walk by, OR every door you walk through lead to school?

Would you rather fight a swarm of robot bees, OR one magic wizard ant?

Would you rather switch bodies with your Mom/Dad for a week and make up the rules at home, OR switch bodies with your teacher for a week and make up the rules at school?

Would you rather slide down the world's tallest waterslide OR ride the world's steepest roller coaster?

Would you rather fart loudly in a crowded room OR silently poop your pants at school?

Would you rather never do homework again, OR get paid $1 million to do someone else's homework, forever?

Would you rather share your biggest secret at a school assembly, OR share a video of all your most embarrassing moments?

Would you rather live in an igloo made of candy OR a mansion made out of pillows?

Would you rather eat as many candy bars as you want, but have to read a book every week, OR watch as many movies as you want, but only eat raw carrots?

Would you rather be punched by a kangaroo OR bitten by a giraffe?

Would you rather decorate your room with slices of turkey as art, OR cover your ceiling in burnt cheese slices?

———◆———

Would you rather have dinner with a wild gorilla OR share a bed with a sneaky tarantula?

Would you rather wear socks made of sandpaper OR wear gloves made of tissue paper?

Would you rather let a worm crawl up your nose OR let a ladybug crawl in your ear?

Would you rather juggle smelly mud balls OR ride a unicycle through slime?

Would you rather chew jalapeño-flavored bubble gum OR eat chocolate-covered habanero peppers?

Would you rather sneeze bubbles OR cry syrup?

Would you rather talk to animals OR read peoples' minds?

Would you rather have your eyes on eyestalks like a snail, OR have 1 big eye like a cyclops?

Would you rather always be sweaty and hot OR always be freezing cold?

Would you rather eat a plate full of flies OR drink a glass of sour milk?

Would you rather have permanent onion breath OR a big pimple on your nose forever?

Would you rather have rows of pointy shark teeth OR two big tusks like a walrus?

Would you rather grow a tail like a mermaid OR grow wings like a fairy?

Would you rather eat a spoonful of hot sauce OR a spoonful of mayonnaise?

Would you rather make a sculpture out of ice cubes OR create a picture out of the trash?

Would you rather make the best chocolate in the world and never be able to eat it, OR make the worst chocolate in the world and eat it all?

Would you rather be an international spy OR a secret ninja?

Would you rather have purple polka dots all over your body OR be striped like a zebra?

Would you rather have to out swim a shark OR out run a cheetah?

Check out our other joke books!

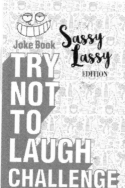

Visit on Amazon Store at:
www.Amazon.com/author/CrazyCorey

Made in the USA
Middletown, DE
15 November 2019